Art Chat

Written by Nicolas Brasch

Contents

Harcourt Achieve

Rigby • Saxon • Steck-Vaughn

www.HarcourtAchieve.com
1.800.531.5015

Chapter Snapshots

Introduction PAGE 4

Artists show us how to see the world in new ways. Sometimes it helps to hear about famous artists and their art from the experts!

1 Italy: Leonardo da Vinci

PAGE 5

Anna interviews an art restorer about Leonardo da Vinci. He was always trying new ways of making art. And not all of his methods worked!

2 China: Terracotta Army of Xi'an PAGE 12

Shang Chou interviews an archaeologist about the Terracotta Army site. It was created over 2000 years ago!

Bartholomew interviews an art critic about Picasso. Picasso is so famous that we only need to use his last name. His art helped us to see the world in a completely new way.

Amy interviews a former student of Emily Carr, a famous Canadian artist. Carr lived and painted in British Columbia during the first half of the twentieth century.

"You can learn more about a work of art by understanding the mood of the artist when it was created."

Introduction

Have you visited an art gallery or museum to look at the work of famous artists?

To understand a work of art, it helps to know something about the artist and *why* they painted certain things or made their art in a particular way. There are many people who know a great deal about art and artists.

Four students met with art experts in different countries to talk about the work they do with their favorite artists' paintings and sculptures.

1 Italy: Leonardo da Vinci

Anna wrote a letter to a big art museum in her city. She wanted to interview someone at the museum who knew a lot about the famous Italian painter and his work. Anna was able to interview an experienced art restorer at the museum.

Leonardo da Vinci

Interview with an Art Restorer

Anna: Thank you for seeing me. I'm sure you are very busy!

Art restorer: I *am* always busy but I'm very pleased to talk to anyone who is interested in art, particularly if they want to hear about my favorite artist, Leonardo da Vinci.

Anna: When did you first become interested in da Vinci's work?

Art restorer: I first saw Leonardo's work when I was a girl. It was such a thrill to see his famous mural. But I saw that the paint seemed damaged and was beginning to flake. Then I learned that some people worked at restoring damaged art works back to their original beauty. I decided that when I grew up, I would learn how to restore works of art. Then people could appreciate the artworks, as they were when they were first done.

Art restorers have added a new tool in the restoration of damaged artworks. Here computer technology is used to assist in returning damaged frescoes to their original state.

Anna: Wow! How do you become an art restorer?

Art restorer: It takes a long time! And you have to be *very* interested in art and artists. At school, I learned all I could about Leonardo da Vinci's drawings, paintings, and murals. Then I went to college and studied for a long time. I have also worked in museums all around the world, learning from other experts how to restore these precious works of art.

Anna: Have you ever seen Leonardo's most famous work, *Mona Lisa*?

Art restorer: Yes, it is my favorite. It is such a beautiful portrait. And it was Leonardo's favorite, too!

Anna: I have only seen pictures of her in books. What do you think makes the *Mona Lisa* such a great work?

Art restorer: It is because of a technique Leonardo used called *sfumato* [**say:** *sfu-ma-to*]. *Sfumato* means "going up in smoke." The technique involves merging different colors to create a smoky effect.

People talk about Mona Lisa's mysterious smile and the look in her eyes. There is a lot of shadow around her mouth and eyes. Leonardo got that effect using *sfumato*. That is the secret of Mona Lisa's mystery.

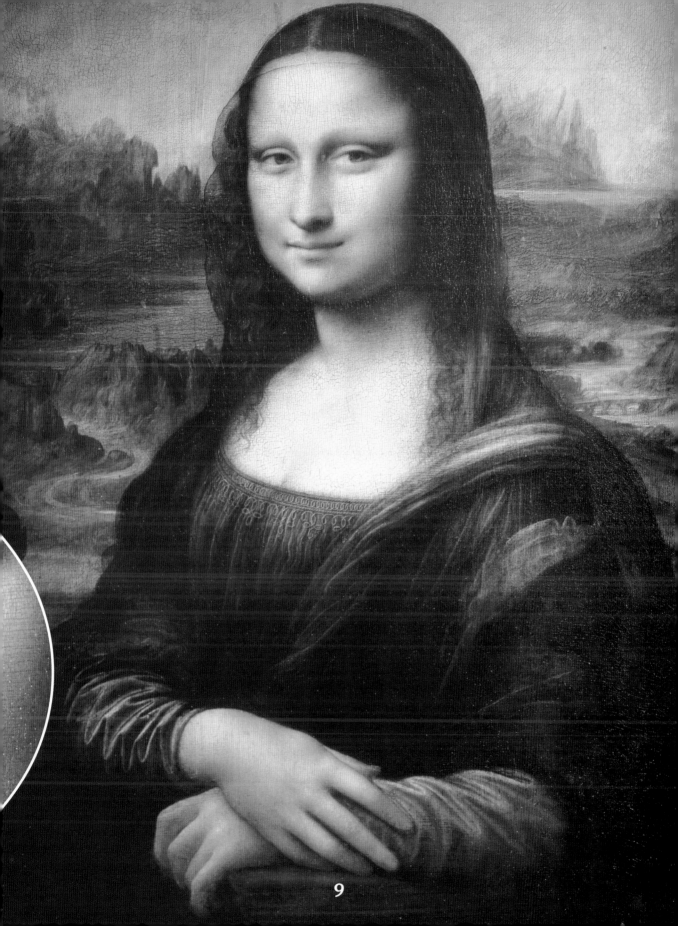

Anna: What about Leonardo's murals? Are they still disintegrating?

Art restorer: Not all of them. But there is a problem with some. Leonardo mixed oil paints with tempera and that was a mistake. Bits of the murals started peeling from the wall as soon as he finished painting.

Anna: Why didn't Leonardo fix them?

Art restorer: Well, he was so busy. He was an artist, a teacher, and an inventor. He went to live in France to work for the king. He was a remarkable man, a genius!

Anna: Thank you so much. Talking to you has made me interested in Leonardo, too.

Artist's File

Name:	Leonardo da Vinci
Date of Birth:	April 15 1452
Place of Birth:	Vinci, Italy
Places of Work:	Florence, Milan, Paris
Favorite Food:	Vegetables
Hobbies:	Reading and writing, particularly about science and medicine

The Renaissance

Leonardo da Vinci lived in a period now known as the Renaissance. It lasted from the 1300s to the 1500s. Renaissance is the French word for re-birth. For painters, writers, and other artists, it was a time to introduce new ideas and methods into their work.

A sketch by
Leonardo da Vinci.

2 China: Terracotta Army of Xi'an

Shang Chou went to Xi'an, China, to visit his grandmother. Before he went, he read about an archaeology student who works at the famous Terracotta Army site. He was lucky enough to be able to meet with him in Xi'an.

A map of China, showing the capital Beijing and the city of Xi'an.

Interview with an Archaeologist

Shang Chou: Thank you for taking time out from work to talk about the Terracotta Army of Xi'an.

Archaeologist: I welcome any chance to talk about the Terracotta Army!

Shang Chou: What are you doing here in Xi'an?

Archaeologist: I'm studying past civilizations at the university. There is still a lot of work to be done on the Terracotta Army site. I am learning so much from the local archaeologists and anthropologists here.

Soldiers from the famous Terracotta Army

Archaeologists and Anthropologists

Archaeologists [say: *ar-kay-ol-o-jists*] and anthropologists are interested in the past. Archaeologists study the remains of cultures, buildings, and tools from the past; anthropologists study people and cultures from the past.

Terracotta

Terracotta (*terra* = earth, *cotta* = baked) is the red-brown, baked clayware found in many places around the world. Roof tiles, garden pots, and many other things are made from terracotta—and, of course, the famous terracotta warriors!

Shang Chou: Can you tell me about the Terracotta Army?

Archaeologist: Yes, but first I'll tell you about the emperor who had them built. He was only 13 when he started the project.

Shang Chou: I guess he just thought of these terracotta soldiers like his toy soldiers.

Archaeologist: Well, he did have quite a lot of them made—in fact nearly 8,000!

Shang Chou: You'd need a big toy box for that many! So, tell me about them.

Artist's File

Full Name:	Emperor Qin Shi Huang
Date of Birth:	259 BC
Place of Birth:	Xi'an
Job:	Emperor of China
Favorite Food:	Rice
Hobbies:	Art, ruling the country

Archaeologist: The Terracotta Army includes chariots, horses, cavalrymen, archers, and foot soldiers. They all have different faces and hairstyles. The emperor had them built as part of his mausoleum, the place where he was going to be buried.

Shang Chou: Why did he want them?

Archaeologist: They were made to remind future generations about the emperor's achievements during his lifetime.

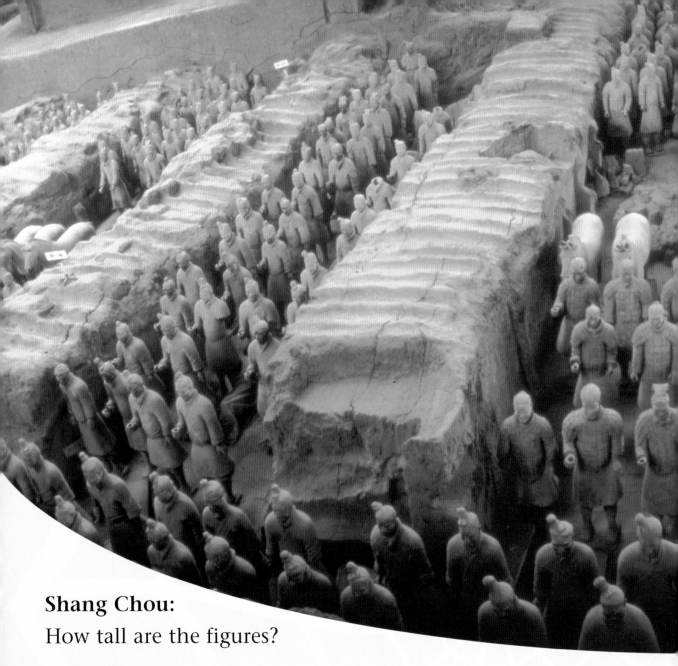

Shang Chou:
How tall are the figures?

Archaeologist: They are life-size. And the weapons they have are real!

Shang Chou: Did only one artist make them?

Archaeologist: No, this was a very big task. Potters from all over the kingdom worked on them. The emperor believed it would be the most important job these artists would ever do.

Shang Chou: I read that these terracotta figures are over 2,000 years old. How have they lasted so long?

Archaeologist: The emperor put a few security features in place to protect them. He had crossbows with arrows fitted into the walls. If someone broke into the mausoleum, they would have set the crossbows off.

Shang Chou: Did anyone break into the mausoleum?

Archaeologist: Not that we know. When the mausoleum was discovered in 1974, the terracotta figures were buried in dust and red earth. Since then, thousands of people have been working every day on the site, brushing the dust away from each figure until it is completely uncovered. Some of the figures were broken and have had to be restored.

Shang Chou: Have you worked on the site?

Archaeologist: Yes I have! There is nothing like first-hand experience. It gives me great excitement to be doing such important work, but it sometimes gives me a backache too!

Shang Chou: Coming here to Xi'an and seeing those long rows and rows of soldiers from thousands of years ago gave me great excitement, too.

The History of Dogs

Chinese scientists were recently involved in a study to determine where dogs originally came from. By studying 654 dogs from five continents, they found that all dogs are very similar and can be traced back to south Asia.

3 France: Pablo Picasso

Bartholomew wants to know more about Pablo Picasso and thought that an art critic might be able to help him. He wrote to a leading expert on Picasso, and was delighted to be granted an interview.

Interview with an Art Critic

Bartholomew: Thank you for allowing me to interview you about Picasso's work. You like Picasso's work very much, don't you?

Art critic: I am a great fan of Picasso's work. My only regret is that he died when I was still a child. I was never able to meet him myself.

Bartholomew: I have always been puzzled about Picasso's work. Perhaps it's just that I don't understand it.

Art critic: Let me try and help you understand his work. I have spent most of my life looking at Picasso's art, as well as reading everything I can about him and his work.

Pablo Picasso

Bartholomew: First, can you tell me how you became an art critic?

Art critic: Well, my father was an art critic, and my mother was a sculptor, so I have always loved art. At first, I worked in an art gallery, and then I started writing articles for art magazines. It took many years for me to build up my knowledge of art, particularly Picasso's work. There are many, many Picasso paintings and sculptures. He lived a long time and he made lots of works of art.

Woman with a Mandolin

Artist's File

Full Name:	Pablo Ruiz Picasso
Date of Birth:	October 25 1881
Place of Birth:	Málaga, Spain
Places of Work:	Spain, France
Favorite Colors:	Blue, brown, green
Hobbies:	Music, animals, observing life

Weeping Woman

The Old Guitarist

Bartholomew: Let's talk about *The Old Guitarist.* I find this painting a little bit sad. Why would an artist paint a picture of a beggar playing a guitar? And Picasso seems to have added to the sad mood by painting the beggar in blue.

Art critic: It's hard to really understand a work of art without understanding the mood of the artist when it was created. Picasso painted *The Old Guitarist* during a time now known as his "Blue Period." He was said to have been sad, and so he used the color blue to express his feelings.

24

Bartholomew: Now I understand that painting a little bit more! How about *Portrait of Ambroise Vollard*? A portrait is supposed to look like someone. This looks nothing like a person!

Art critic: You need to have an open mind when you look at art. A portrait is an artist's impression of the subject. It doesn't have to be realistic.

Bartholomew: That's a good point.

Portrait of Ambroise Vollard

Art critic:
I suppose you don't like *Mandolin*, which Picasso created in 1914?

Bartholomew:
To me, *Mandolin* is just a few pieces of wood glued together!

Mandolin

Art critic: Works of art should be considered alongside the artist's other work. With *Mandolin*, Picasso was trying to create a sculpture that was similar to paintings he was creating at that time. So which of Picasso's works do you like the least?

Bartholomew: That would have to be *Composition with a Sliced Pear*. It's just so boring! What's interesting about a slice of pear?

Art critic: There is beauty in everything. That's the point. A slice of pear has as much relevance in art as a portrait of a beautiful woman, or a watercolor of the sea.

Bartholomew: Hmmm. I guess we'll just have to agree to disagree.

Composition with a Sliced Pear

Critics Using Technology

Critics sometimes argue about whether a certain writer wrote a particular book, poem, or play. Today, computer software programs can be used to examine a writer's complete works. The program identifies common phrases used throughout all the works and helps the critics discover the real writer of works that are in question.

4 Canada: Emily Carr

Artist's File

Name of Artist:	Emily Carr
Date of Birth:	December 13 1871
Place of Birth:	Victoria, British Columbia, Canada
Inspiration:	The land and indigenous culture along the Canadian Pacific coast
Favorite Materials:	Oil paint and gasoline
Hobbies:	Writing, walking through wilderness

Amy is a fan of Emily Carr, one of Canada's best known artists and writers. Carr influenced many up-and-coming artists. Here, Amy speaks to an artist who was taught as a student by Emily Carr.

Interview with an Artist

Amy: Thank you so much for agreeing to talk to me. You studied under Emily Carr when you were an art student?

Artist: Yes, I did. It was a very long time ago, but it was one of the most interesting times of my life. Emily Carr was one of my heroes.

Amy: I have just read a book by Emily Carr called *Klee Wyck*. Why did she call it that?

Artist: "Klee Wyck" was a nickname given to her by the Nuu-Chah-Nulth people. It means "Laughing One."

Amy: How important were the Nuu-Chah-Nulth people in influencing Emily Carr's art?

Artist: Very important. Both their culture and their land feature in many of her paintings and books.

British Columbia

British Columbia is one of the 10 provinces that make up the country of Canada. British Columbia covers 357,200 square miles in the west of Canada. It includes the Pacific coast. Today, over four million people live in British Columbia. The major cities in British Columbia are Vancouver and Victoria.

Amy: She lived and worked in Canada, France, England, and the United States. She must have moved around a lot.

Artist: Yes, but she was proudly Canadian. There is a wonderful thing she said that I always remember. Let me read it to you: "It is wonderful to feel the grandness of Canada in the raw, not because she is Canada but because she's something sublime that you were born into, some great rugged power that you are a part of."

Amy: That's truly beautiful. Thank you for remembering your time with Emily Carr and sharing it with me.

Photograph of an Emily Carr painting featuring the land and/or culture of the Nuu-Chah-Nulth people

Index

Bookweb Links

Key to Bookweb Fact Boxes
- ■ **Arts**
- ■ **Health**
- ■ **Science**
- ■ **Social Studies**
- ■ **Technology**

Read more Bookweb 4 books about art and artists:

Artists' Choice—Nonfiction